DONALD TRUMP PRESENTS:

DONALD TRUMP'S

A DONALD TRUMP CHRISTMAS CAROL

BEING
A Ghost Story of Democracy

PUBLISHED BY CROOKED PENGUIN

&

THE FAILING EBURY PRESS

EBURY
PRESS

1 3 5 7 9 10 8 6 4 2

Ebury Press, an imprint of Ebury Publishing
20 Vauxhall Bridge Road
London SW1V 2SA

Ebury Press is part of the Penguin Random House group of companies
whose addresses can be found at global.penguinrandomhouse.com

Penguin
Random House
UK

First published by Ebury Press in 2017

www.penguin.co.uk

A CIP catalogue record for this book is available from the British Library

ISBN 9781785037863

Edited by Anna Mrowiec

Printed and bound in Great Britain by Clays Ltd, St Ives PLC

Penguin Random House is committed to a sustainable future for
our business, our readers and our planet. This book is made from
Forest Stewardship Council® certified paper.

To the people of the United States.
You had a good run.

CONTENTS

STAVE I

Nixon's Ghost

Trump was president: of that there could be no doubt. President of the United States, no less! And not just any United States — the United States of America! Read it again, for familiarity can dull even the strangest of facts: Trump was president. If I awoke tomorrow to find a face growing out of my abdomen, which then introduced itself as Mr Lionel Caruthers, I daresay I might eventually come to accept his friends stooping before me and bellowing: 'Yo, Lionel, whassup?!' That said, I do not think I shall ever be free of a shuddering disbelief when reading any article that deploys the words 'President Trump'. Such incredulity notwithstanding, the fact remains that an election had been called and Trump had won.

Mind! I do not mean to say that he won in the sense of securing the greatest number of votes.

No, Trump had failed to achieve a majority of popular support, losing by a margin of some three million. Myself, I might have deemed this an insuperable obstacle to victory, but the framers of the U.S. constitution thought otherwise, and who am I to doubt the wisdom of those syphilitic slave-owners? The ballots had been cast, the arms of the voting machines tugged, and the chads left to hang. As that grim night had unfolded, the electoral college had proved as worthless an educational establishment as Trump University. The preening orange monster was elevated and his opponent — that pantsuit-wearing elitist! — laid low. Through his fame and fortune, and possibly a little help from an army of Russian hackers, he had — more or less fairly — been elected. To the venerable roster that bore the names George Washington, Abraham Lincoln and Franklin Delano Roosevelt, the name of Ebenezer Trump was now irrevocably added.

Trump! The implausibly coiffed game-show host! The butt of easy jokes on late night television! The remorseless braggart, the deplorable racist, the inveterate and self-confessed grabber of pussy! This was the man who now commanded the world's last superpower, the man whose stubby forefinger hovered over the nuclear button. Dear reader, at the risk of sounding like a broken record (or, to be more modern, a faulty MP3), I must repeat: Trump was president. This was the case when he was inaugurated — twentieth of January, year of our Lord two thousand and seventeen — and it was still the case on the twenty-fourth of December, the date our story takes place.

Christmas Eve, and the town of Washington D.C. was beset with a cruel and unyielding winter. Did it snow? My friend, there was snow in abundance: a surfeit of snow, an excess of snow, a great, greedy glut of snow! Snow fell on the Capitol Building, which was empty, for the senators and congressmen had each gone home to at least one of their families. Snow blanketed the National Mall, where previously some two billion souls had gathered to watch Trump's swearing in (that was, according to Trump). Snow settled on the brows of the shivering homeless, who merited no discussion in the corridors of power, for they could not afford to hire lobbyists. And amid all this whirling whiteness stood the White House, in whose Oval Office sat President Trump. Old Trump took no notice of the winter waltz being conducted outside; men of his sort have no time for snowflakes. Anyway, he was occupied with a matter far weightier than Yuletide precipitation. The president, as you may have guessed, was tweeting.

Ebenezer Trump tweeted:
The FAKE NEWS media says I'm a 'miser'. I'm the least miserly person you ever met. HUMBUG!
10.45 — 24 Dec 2017

No sooner had he pressed 'send' than his mentions were flooded with a thousand eager voices. Yes, there were the usual cries of 'LIAR!' and 'RESIGN!', but also a great deal of approbation — mostly from Moldovan robots and teenagers whose profile picture was a frog. This was all the same to Trump, for he did not care what kind of response he got, so long as it was huge. Magnitude was the only thing Trump valued. Indeed, the word 'huge' was insufficiently huge for him, and so he built several storeys upon the adjective, elongating it to 'yoooooooooooge'. Soon Trump felt the itch of self-expression once more. He did not necessarily have anything to say, but he would be damned if that stopped him.

Ebenezer Trump tweeted:

Christmas is for losers. You call it a present, I call it a handout. SAD! #MAGA #humbug

10.47 — 24 Dec 2017

It was a spirited effort, though perhaps not up there with his finest (recent successes had included 'Nobody in the history of the universe has been treated more unfairly than Trump' and 'Penguins. Gay? We have a right to know'). Nonetheless, he seemed satisfied, leaning back in his chair and placing his feet upon the desk where JFK once sat.

But, oh, he was a wretched specimen of greed, was Trump! A grasping, clutching, conniving, bellicose, venal, vile, insensible old sinner! In him, nature had combined the body of a seventy-one-year-old with the mind of a toddler, misplacing in the process that innocence and joy one might have expected of the latter party. Trump's genius was to make the ludicrous lucrative, and thus he sold himself. For ludicrous he was: a gaudy, grandiloquent clown of a man! His hair was incredible, in the sense that no sane person would credit it: a helmet of hardened candy floss, drawn across his scalp in contravention of Nature's will; the corpse of an abandoned poodle; a strenuously engineered monument to vanity!

His face, curdled long ago into an expression of pugnacious stupidity, was a shade of bronze not to be found anywhere else on his milk-white physique. Indeed, it was as if he were a latter-day Achilles, whose mother, dipping her infant into a Styx of fake-tan, had not bothered to proceed beyond the neckline. His constant squint and puckered mouth seemed an attempt to shut out the world, to guard against any light or goodness that might have entered therein. Oh, how he scrunched himself up, like an ancient child, forever trapped in his initial tantrum!

Moving down, one found a pair of tiny, twitching hands, which yearned to defy their limited dimensions by grabbing anything and everything that life had to offer. I shall not speculate as to the dimensions of any other appendage, but suffice it to say that Trump wore a long, blood-red tie, which hung between his legs, and grazed the floor in a manner that might have caused Dr Freud to choke on his cigar.

Alas this clownish anatomy was but an overture to the interminable opera of his deficiencies!

However deranged his appearance, Trump's personality surpassed it quite. His heart was as cold as the wind outside, and his words as false as his hair. Did Trump lie? My good fellow, to call Trump a liar would be to call Mike Tyson a bloke who could hold his own in a fight. He was the Mozart of mendacity and the Hogarth of hogwash; the Shakespeare of slander and the Liberace of libel; the Fibonacci of fibs and the Picasso of the porky pie. Lies escaped his lips like convicts from a sundered jail. He would tell you that up was down and black was white; that every Muslim was a terrorist and every Mexican a rapist; that the sun set in the East and that Trump steaks were edible. Most frequently of all, he would tell you that he was the smartest, the strongest, the richest, the classiest, and the most beloved of anyone, anywhere. So confident was Trump in his contradictions, so bullish in his bullshit, that it was an enduring mystery whether he himself believed the nonsense he spouted.

In truth, it was a moot point, for honesty and falsehood are only meaningful if one has respect for one's listener, and this Trump lacked entirely. By his reckoning, all of mankind fell into the category of either winners or losers, and there could only be one winner: Trump. No prize could be achieved, but that it was wrenched from the grasp of a lesser man; no woman could be wooed, but that she was conquered and made submissive; no joy could be felt, but that another must suffer. Unless Trump remained forever on top, he feared he would be subsumed by the darkness within.

This conviction informed both his bizarre mode of speech and his obscene lifestyle, for Trump existed in a land of hyperbole, of super tremendous perfection, of very classy, record-breaking ultra-luxury. In terms of interior decorating, he had but one idea: gold, gold and yet more gold. He gleefully bought up a profusion of gold chairs, gold tables, gold taps and gold toilets. He did so shamelessly, for Trump felt never felt guilty when it came to gilt. Indeed, his apartment in New York was so plastered with gold leaf that the dimmest of lights would set the place ablaze. Thus Trump proved that old wives' tale, for these carats could indeed help you see in the dark. According to one popular rumour, he had even gone so far as to invest in a golden shower.

And yet for all this lavish spending, Trump would rather have performed his own vasectomy with a wooden spoon than waste a penny on others. There was no contractor he would not stiff, no ex-wife he would not sue into insolvency, no charity gala he would not attend in order to scoff their hors d'oeuvres and grin for their cameras, before fleeing when the time came for donations. It never once occurred to him that he might enrich his existence by enriching the existence of others. The private jet, the model wife, the golden tower bearing his name — these were, to Trump, the markers of a life well lived. Generosity was mere weakness and to be humble betrayed a lack of testosterone. Humanity was his plaything, and the world one big pudendum to grab ('when you're a star, they let you do it'). This, I fear, was the measure of the man: he was a rutting pig, indifferent to the world's cries; a modern monster, hooked on instant and empty pleasures; a tangerine-hued tyrant, bewigged and belligerent! In short, he was the meanest, dumbest son-of-a-bitch you ever did see.

Given Trump's contempt for his fellow man, it is perhaps understandable that his preferred method of communication should be Twitter. By use of this app, he could dispense his words from on high, as though he were the God of the Old Testament and sent poor Moses down Sinai, bearing a brace of misspelled tablets. He loved to hurl a grenade among the pigeons, and it was this activity that engrossed him when he heard the sound of someone entering his office. Trump glanced up from his screen and spotted the figure of a woman. He allowed his eyes to travel up her long legs, her curving hips and breasts, and the primped perfection of her lustrous blonde hair. Finally, they alighted upon the woman's face, and he realised that it was his daughter, Ivanka.

Trump was pleased to see her, for Ivanka was his favourite child (and, indeed, favourite woman). However, his customary leer collapsed as she stepped forward and, with a beaming smile, cried 'Merry Christmas, father!'

'What's that?' Trump replied. 'Merry Christmas? I don't see what's so merry about it. There's nothing good on TV and everybody's talking about love and peace instead of what they should be talking about, which is me. Any fool who goes around saying Merry Christmas should be locked up in jail with Crooked Hillary.'

'Perhaps,' said his daughter. 'Nevertheless, I invite you to spend the day with me, Jared and the kids.'

At this, Trump's frown turned into a scowl.

'Why would I want to celebrate Christmas?' he groused. 'I'm not a Christian. What, they expect me to believe in some guy called God who's more of a big shot than me? Please.'

'All the more reason to come,' Ivanka persisted, 'for Jared and I are Jewish, and won't be celebrating! It shall be a communal rather than a religious gathering, an opportunity to bask in fellow feeling and familial warmth! A chance to dandle your grandchild on your lap as you while away the eve in the company of those closest to you!'

'Eh, pass,' said Trump.

His daughter was stung. For all that she marketed herself as a feminist, the fact is that Ivanka craved nothing more in life than her father's approval (approval, that is to say, of the non-physical variety).

'Come now,' she beseeched, 'this is the one time of year we all join together and embrace —'

'Look, honey,' Trump snapped, 'you've got a dynamite body, but, I hate to say it, not much going on up here.'

(At this, he tapped a stumpy finger against his great, balloon-like head.)

'If I've told you once, I've told you a thousand times: Christmas sucks. We're talking humbug, bigly.'

'But father —'

'You spend Christmas how you want, I'll spend it how I want: playing golf, then sitting at home, shouting at the TV whenever someone brown comes on.'

A look of sadness flashed across Ivanka's features, but was quickly replaced by her Stepfordian smile.

'Well, Daddy,' she ventured, 'I can see I am as powerless to change your mind as I was in regard to the Paris Agreement. However you choose to spend this Noel, I hope it brings you comfort and joy.'

With that, she turned to leave, affording Ebenezer one last, appreciative look at her behind.

Once she had gone, Trump reflected that he had been a little tough on the girl. He resolved to make it up to her; perhaps he would tweet a presidential decree that all patriotic Americans should buy the Ivanka Trump Jewellery Collection. However, before he could return to molesting his Samsung, a sheepish figure entered the room. It was his aide, Bob Cratchit, and Trump regarded the man with beady, ungenerous eyes.

'What do *you* want?' he growled.

'Begging your pardon, sir,' replied Mr Cratchit, 'but, seeing as it's getting towards eleven, I thought I might head home to the family.'

'I've never let you leave early before,' said Trump. 'Why would I do that now?'

'Why, sir, because it's Christmas Eve.'

'And that gives you the right to slack off?' Trump cried. 'Good God, what am I paying you for?'

Bob might have answered that he was scarcely paid at all, being yet another victim of Trump's parsimony, but he opted for a judicious silence.

'Un-believable,' Trump continued. 'I'm guessing you want tomorrow off as well?'

'If that's quite convenient, Mr President,' replied Cratchit.

'Like hell is it convenient!' Trump thundered. 'Who's going to fluff my pillows? Act as my footstool? Fill Mike Pence's bowl with that dog food he likes?'

Bob assured his boss that he would attend to these duties on the twenty-sixth, and come in early to do so. Eventually Trump consented to his leaving, on the strict condition that Bob was not to have any fun, and must spend Christmas Day watching reruns of *The Apprentice*. The aide agreed, then darted out the Oval Office as fast as might be considered seemly. Trump sighed and, deciding to call it a night, slouched his way towards the Residence.

'Christmas!' Trump hissed to himself as he ascended the stairs. 'Humbug!' What made the day so special, he wondered. What right had his underlings to take liberties, just because, however many years ago, some kid was born in the Middle East? If Jesus were alive today, Trump mused, he would put him on a no-fly list and the world would be better for it!

He arrived at the door to his quarters and reached for the knob. It was a wholly unremarkable knob, one that Trump had seen and turned every night he had spent at the White House (which were not that many, given his frequent trips to Mar-a-Lago). Nothing more than your standard brass number, with lined mortice and hinged escutcheon plate. Now, the reader may well wonder why I have squandered their time on so exhaustive a description of an entirely mediocre piece of metalwork. I do so merely to confirm that this was a resolutely normal item, one which had never displayed any inclination towards the surreal or supernatural. That now being established, can any man explain to me how it happened that Trump, mere milliseconds from grasping said doorknob, saw not a doorknob, but the face of Hillary Clinton?

Hillary's face! The piercing blue eyes, the micromanaged hairdo, the wrinkles that spoke of a lifetime harangued by male inadequates. It glared up at Trump reproachfully, as silent as a glass ceiling that had failed to shatter. He started back in fear. Hillary had always frightened him. Her power, her connections, all those facts and figures at her command. In many ways, she was Trump's greatest nightmare — a woman his own age, entirely ungrabbable, who sometimes dispensed with makeup entirely. Horrible!

Worst of all, she had denied him victory in the popular vote, blurring the line between winner and loser in a way that made Trump feel queasy. But no! Hillary had not really won — those were illegal voters, paid for by Hollywood liberals and the Elders of Zion. This must have been the case, for, if a fact made Trump look less majestic, then it simply could not be true. So lost was he in these musings that he did not notice the point at which the doorknob ceased to bear the face of his rival and resumed its former appearance. Yet this must have happened, for there it stood, gleaming in the half-light, as ordinary as ever, with Hillary nowhere to be seen. 'Humbug,' Trump muttered, and went inside.

Though much alarmed by this vision, Trump was soon able to put it out of his mind (such are the advantages of a three-second attention span). He shrugged off his jacket, loosened his prodigious tie, and was soon changed into his nocturnal garb of dressing gown, slippers and nightcap. Thus attired, he sank into the high-backed chair that faced his eighty-inch plasma screen, and began to channel surf.

Trump clicked through *World's Dumbest Plumbers*, *Celebrity Holocaust Denial*, and a sitcom about three clones forced to move back in with their parent (a test tube), before settling on a reality show that some waggish executive had entitled *S.T. Island*. The central conceit of the programme was to deposit a horde of attractive twenty-somethings on a remote landmass, then record as they all had sex with one another. To add intrigue to the proceedings, each contestant started off with a different STI and was able to win prizes by correctly guessing who had given them what. Trump liked reality television — as well he might, for it had afforded him the platform to attain his current position. He leaned back in his chair, momentarily at peace with the world. However, just as Dessandra was about to reveal whether she believed Vinnie or Pauly Q had given her that herpes, the room was filled with an unholy cry.

Jolted from his reverie, Trump turned off the TV and focused on the unfamiliar sound. 'Arrrrr-rrooooooooooo…' it went, 'arrrrrrroooooooooooooo!'

Underscoring this mournful noise was a great clanking of chains, and the thud of footsteps drawing near. Trump leaned forward, and his fingers clenched upon the armrest, creating a series of tiny dents.

'Bob?' he called out. 'Ivanka? Wait a minute, is this some prank-show thing? If I'm being Punk'd, I swear to God—'

He froze, for at that moment he perceived a figure rising through the floorboards, transparent and draped in chains. Moaning at the weight of its burden, the spectre shambled across the room, until finally it stood before the seated Trump. He peered

at the ghastly apparition: its darting eyes, its five-o'-clock shadow, its hangdog look of paranoia; they were all unmistakeable. That this was the ghost of Richard Nixon would be obvious to even the meanest intellect.

'Who the hell are you?' asked Trump.

'Foolish man,' replied the shade. 'Ask me instead who I was.'

'Whatever,' Trump said. 'Who were you, then?'

'I was Richard Milhous Nixon, thirty-seventh president of the United States.'

'Right, so you're from, like, the 1800s?'

'What?' exclaimed the Ghost, suddenly more irritated than ominous. 'How can you fail to know who I am? You were twenty-three when I was elected. I opened trade relations with China. I was the only president ever to resign, for Christ's sake!'

'Still not ringing any bells.'

The Spirit looked vexed, for it could sense this haunting would be harder than anticipated.

Trump ploughed on: 'Listen, I'm not a historian. All I know is, if you don't scram, I'll call the Secret Service and have you thrown in jail.'

'Oh, but I am already in jail,' replied the spectre. 'A jail more awful than any this earth may boast.'

'I dunno,' said Trump, 'I hear jail can be pretty nasty. Some of them don't even do room service.'

'No mortal hand may restrain me,' the Ghost intoned, 'for I am not of this realm. I am cursed to roam a world in which I may take no succour, for I am neither alive nor dead.'

Neither alive nor dead? That sounded ambiguous, and Trump did not care for nuance. As far as he was concerned, everything was either tremendous or terrible, classy or trash, a gorgeous dame or a disgusting dog.

'OK, nuh-uh, not buying it.'

'Eh?' said the shade of Nixon. 'What aren't you buying?'

'All this ghost crap. Totally unbelievable.'

'You would deny the evidence of your own senses?'

'I see crazy crap all the time,' Trump returned. 'My doctor says it's cos the only exercise I do is golf and my diet's horrible. Seriously, just this evening I had a bucket of KFC, a well-done steak with ketchup, and a double helping of chocolate ice cream. For all I know, you could be an undigested bit of chicken.'

At this, Nixon let out a howl that chilled Trump to the marrow.

'Fine!' he cried. 'You're real, I get it. So what do you want from me?'

'We're not so different, you and I,' rumbled the Ghost. 'Lying to the public, holding weird grudges, degrading the office of president ... To be fair to myself, I was way smarter and never once appeared on *WrestleMania*, but still. The path you are embarked upon, Ebenezer, shall lead to impeachment and, worse, your eternal damnation. That is the path I chose and, though it is too late for me, I would give you the chance to escape my fate.'

Trump squinted at the great chain that wound about the ghoul: its links were thick and rusty, and, where one might expect to see a ball, there dangled a large, old-fashioned tape recorder.

'So what's with the chain?' said Trump. 'Are you one of those rappers they have nowadays? Gotta say, you don't look black.'

The Ghost hung his head and unleashed a wail of anguish.

'These are the links I forged in life. The links I am cursed to wear forevermore. O, woe is me! I forged them through my lies, my cheating, my corruption. Now I languish below, being interviewed by David Frost for all eternity! Arrrrooooooooooo!'

Trump sat back in his chair, unimpressed.

'OK, no offence? Sounds like you're a real bozo. Some people feel sorry for the damned; me, I like people who were never damned.'

The Ghost smiled, grimly.

'Bozo I may be, Ebenezer, but you are forging quite the chain for yourself. Far longer than mine, it is. Longer, even, than your ties.'

Trump glanced down in spite of himself, half expecting to see some fifty or sixty fathoms of golden cable, coiled at his feet like a vast, metallic snake. For the first time, he felt a pang of honest dread. It was as though icy waters were rising in the black cave of his chest.

'Say I don't feel like getting damned,' he ventured, 'who do I pay off?'

'Your trifling coin has no currency where I reside,' the Ghost responded. 'Nevertheless, I have secured you assistance.'

'Phew,' said Trump, 'glad that's taken care of. Well, I should get some shut-eye — night night!'

'You will be haunted,' resumed the Ghost, 'by three Spirits.'

Trump's face fell.

'Listen, Dick, bit of constructive criticism: ghosts? Too scary. Not the kind of help I was hoping for, at all.'

'Your preferences are of no concern,' the Ghost declared. 'Heed these spirits, Ebenezer Trump, for they shall show you the error of your ways.'

At this, Trump jutted out his lower jaw, and defiance flared in his narrow eyes.

'Yeah, well, my ways can't be that wrong, cos I'm the president, OK? I think I'm doing pretty good.'

Nixon's Ghost merely stared back at him, then began to walk away. He sank into the floorboards and, with a great cry of 'I AM NOT A SPOOK!', he was gone.

Trump had been shaken by these events and, try as he might, was unable to emit even the softest 'humbug'. Exhausted, he clambered into bed, but the words of his ghostly visitor still lingered. So Trump did what older Americans generally do when troubled by thoughts of mortality: he switched on Fox News.

Sitting behind the desk was a middle-aged man with a shiny suit and Brylcreemed hair, whose voice quivered in outrage. Beneath him, a chyron screamed 'BREAKING: MUSLIMS HIJACK SANTA'S SLEIGH'.

'My God,' Trump mumbled to himself. 'Bad dudes. Not good.'

The newsreader held forth on these vicious Islamists, pausing only to inveigh against their politically correct defenders. Some of those bleeding hearts even went so far as to claim that Santa did not exist!

'Typical!' Trump yawned. 'We need to get smart, or we'll be overrun, just like the North Pole.'

The newsreader then turned to a woman with golden, lacquered hair, who smiled and simpered and agreed with everything that he had said. There was indeed a War on Christmas, and the only rational solution was stricter controls on immigration; the Democrats and the Hollywood elite had supported Muslamic terror squads for too long.

'Too long,' Trump murmured, sinking back upon his pillow.

The newsreader nodded frantically at his female counterpart, who was almost certainly named either Meghan or Ashley. He added that the legislation surrounding this issue was too soft and needed to get hard quick.

'Get hard,' the president repeated.

Comforted by this alternate reality of manly men, obliging blondes and anonymous brown-skinned aggressors, Trump soon found himself drifting into a deep and dreamless sleep.

STAVE II

The First of the Three Spirits

Trump was woken by the blaring of a horn, and opened his eyes to find the room flooded with light. At the centre of this incandescence stood the music's originator: a grey-suited, white-haired man, grooving away on the saxophone. Squinting even harder than usual, Trump was able make out the apparition, who put his instrument to one side, did a thumbs up, then bit his lower lip.

'Bill Clinton?!' Trump spluttered.

'Well, hey there,' the Spirit replied in an Arkansan drawl, 'sorry to intrude. This isn't my first time surprising someone in the middle of the night, though it's usually not a dude, if you catch my drift.'

'What the hell are you doing here?' said Trump.

'I thought Nixon told you: I'm the first of the three spirits, the Ghost of Christmas Past.'

'But Bill,' exclaimed Trump, 'you aren't dead! Aren't ghosts supposed to be dead?'

'Sure,' the Spirit replied, 'and presidents aren't supposed to get BJs in the Oval Office, but I make my own rules.'

The Ghost regarded the room with a look of fond remembrance.

'Man, if these walls could talk … That would be a real problem for me. Anyway, how are you finding the place?'

'Eh,' said Trump, 'if I'm honest, not fantastic. This building's horrible, no class. I keep saying "Why settle for a White House? Can't we make it a Gold House?" You'd think they'd at least let me install a jacuzzi in the Rose Garden, but no. Then there's all the losers and haters saying I'm a bad president, when I'm clearly the best one there's ever been. And don't get me started on the Fake News Media, making me look like an idiot by reporting what I say — unfair, bigly. Cos the thing is, I don't need this crappy job. I mean, come on, I'm Ebenezer Trump, the ultimate American success story. These guys should be grateful I agreed to be their king, or whatever …'

The Spirit shook his head and his aura took on a darker hue.

'Goddamn, you are one needy son-of-a-bitch, aren't you? D'you ever wonder how you ended up like this?'

'What's there to wonder about?' said Trump. 'I'm a self-made man: I started with nothing but the shirt on my back and a small, multi-million-dollar loan from my father.'

'Self-made man, huh?' said the Spirit. 'Well, I'm here to unmake you. You and I are going on a little road trip ... '

Here the spirit's smile turned from sheepish to wolfish, and Trump felt himself grow nervous.

'Don't wanna,' he murmured, in a voice much smaller than usual.

Just then, the room's high windows shot open, as though of their own accord. The Spirit produced a blue dress, curiously stained, which he began to whirl around his head like a helicopter blade. He seized Trump's hand and, in an instant, the pair flew out through the window and into the blizzarding sky.

In but a heartbeat, the myriad lights of D.C. were spread beneath them. There was the Washington Monument, the Smithsonian, the Lincoln Memorial! There was the Capitol Building, that sacred temple of democracy, bedecked with purest snow!

'Hell of a view, isn't it?' exclaimed the Spirit.

By way of reply, Trump vomited, and down went his evening repast of steak, ice cream and KFC (regrettably, this happened just as they flew over Arlington National Cemetery). Fortunately, he did not have to endure the trip very long, for within seconds the buildings below had been replaced with the skyscrapers of New York City ...

As they came to land upon a bustling street, Trump was shocked to observe that it was now daytime and his surroundings were eerily familiar.

'We're in Queens,' he mused aloud, 'but something's different ...'

In a milkshake parlour opposite, a group of young people were doing the jitterbug to Elvis Presley's 'Hound Dog'. Two pregnant ladies strolled by, smoking cigarettes and discussing their husbands, who hadn't been the same since returning from Korea. The Spirit nudged Trump and indicated an old-timey paperboy in flat cap and shorts.

'Extree, extree!' he cried. 'Dwight D. Eisenhower named Man of 1956, which is the year this is!'

After a long pause while he puzzled over the scene in front of him, Trump eventually turned to the spirit. 'What the hell? Why've you brought me back to the fifties?'

'Well, you've brought the country back to the fifties,' replied the Ghost. 'Besides, this isn't any old day; it's Christmas Day, 1956. Remember it?'

'I don't like to remember things,' said Trump. 'It makes my brain go icky and my stomach feel weird. Plus, if I remembered stuff, I'd have to, like, keep the promises I make. No thank you.'

'Oh, but surely you recall this scene,' the Ghost insisted and, with a sweep of his arm, indicated a father and son traversing the sidewalk. The parent strode along in his greatcoat and trilby – one vast, moustachioed scowl. The fair-haired child scrambled after him, ten years of age and clutching a lollipop in his tiny hand.

'Shake a leg, Ebenezer!' cried the father. 'I have business to attend to, and you're moving as slow as a goddamn Spaniard!'

Trump turned to the Spirit, his tangerine face lit up with excitement.

'Oh boy!' he exclaimed. 'That's my dad. Dad! DAD!'

'They can't see us,' admonished the Ghost. 'These are but the shadows of what was.'

'Shame,' said Trump. 'Would've been great to talk to him. Dad was the best guy. My hero. Incredible businessman, truly.'

'Ah yes,' said the Spirit. 'Let's observe the businessman in action ...'

The Ghost took Trump's arm, his grip gentle but inexorable, and together they floated to the fifth floor of a tenement building, whose wall they passed through as if it were air. Now the two stood in a dank corridor, with lights a-flicker and a carpet alive with insects. Before them were the father and son, the former hammering his fist against the door of apartment 21B.

'Keep your wits about you, boy,' said Trump Senior, 'these folk are Irish, and everybody knows the Hibernian skull shape predisposes one to violence.'

'Sure thing, Pops,' replied Trump Junior, with a look of awed adoration.

The door was answered by a skinny fellow with kind, imploring eyes.

'Mr Trump!' the man gasped. 'It's a pleasure to see you.'

'We both know that's bunk,' replied his grim visitor. 'I certainly wouldn't be pleased to see the man I owed *five dollars* in unpaid rent ...'

'Your daddy was a slumlord?' the Spirit enquired of Ebenezer.

'Sure,' Trump responded, 'but these were *Trump* slums — the classiest, most luxurious slums around!'

'Forgive me, sir,' said the trembling tenant, 'but work has been scarce since the pickle factory exploded. Perhaps you might show my family some lenience, given the holy season?'

'Lenience?' Trump's father cried. 'Simply because it happens to be the twenty-fifth day of December? Humbug!'

The tenant gulped, then stiffened his resolve.

'With all due respect, sir, the fault is not entirely ours. It's mighty hard to make ends meet when you're constantly falling through rotten floorboards, or being woken at 4am by rat fights. Perhaps you might see your way to bringing this building up to code?'

At this, Trump Senior grabbed the poor fellow's lapels and pinned him against the doorframe.

'The day I do that,' he hissed, 'is the day I rent one of these apartments to a Negro! You'll give me that money and you'll give me it now!'

'But—but sir,' the man pleaded. 'I had hoped to provide my family with a small meal to mark the occasion!'

At this, the landlord's face grew so red it looked for all the world as though his moustache had been relocated to a bowl of Bolognese.

'Goddammit,' he yelled, 'I'll see you kicked out on the street or my name isn't Frederick Christ Trump, which it is! Genuinely, my middle name is Christ — look it up!'

Young Ebenezer licked his lollipop, expressionless, as the tenant handed over his tattered banknotes. These Trump pocketed with a smile of dark satisfaction.

'Pleasure doing business with you.'

He spun on his heel and strode on, with little Ebenezer scurrying to keep up. The Spirit turned to Trump.

'That must have been tough for a kid,' he said, in a gentle voice. 'How did it make you feel?'

'Feel?' Trump replied. 'It made me feel great. Honoured to watch a master at work.'

The Spirit grasped Trump's sleeve and they floated up through several ceilings before arriving at another corridor, just as repugnant as its downstairs cousin. Once again, Frederick and Ebenezer stood beside a dilapidated threshold. The boy licked his lollipop as the father explained that these next tenants were a family of Mexicans, twelve weeks behind on their rent.

'Horrible,' said young Ebenezer, though his heart wasn't in it. 'Bad hombres, not good.'

'Because they refuse to pay,' continued his father, 'that means they have to be evicted. I want you to do so, and get a feel for the business.'

Young Ebenezer froze, mid-lick, then lowered his lollipop.

'D-Daddy, I don't think I—'

But Frederick was already rapping his knuckles against the door. A moment later, it opened to reveal a young Latina, cradling her infant tenderly.

'Good morning,' boomed the elder Trump. 'I'm your landlord, and my son here has something he'd like to say to you. Take it away, boy.'

'Um … Er …' said the child, the lolly hanging limp by his side.

'What is it, *cariño*?' the mother said with a smile, 'You can tell me.'

'You heard that, kid?' said his father. 'She wants to know.'

'I—I … Well, the thing is, you see …'

The words kept failing his boyish tongue. Once again, the woman gave an encouraging smile: 'Is something the matter, *mijo*?'

'Out with it, damn you!' said Frederick Christ Trump.

Ebenezer glanced from the woman to his father, then his father to the woman, and, all of a sudden, a single tear darted down his cheek. Horror spread across his father's features.

'My God,' he exclaimed. 'Are you crying?'

'No!' the boy lied.

Frederick put his face so close to young Ebenezer's that the child could feel the very bristles of his moustache.

'I brought you out here so you could prove yourself a man,' he growled. 'Instead, you start crying like some kind of Argentinian! You don't deserve the name Trump! You're nothing but a loser! A pussy! Sad!'

As the puce-faced tyrant continued to scream, Trump — our Trump — rounded on the Spirit.

'OK, that's enough! So my dad was rough once or twice. That's what made me the man I am today. I'm bored of this, I want to go someplace else!'

'Very well,' replied the Spirit.

The walls around them seemed to dissolve and reform in an instant, and Trump found himself in a large, trendy nightclub, thronged with revellers. Nearby, two women with enormous afros and flared jeans danced to Donna Summer, while discussing their boyfriends, who hadn't been the same since they got home from Vietnam. Trump spotted a familiar figure standing in the corner of the room: it was the paperboy, now in his mid-thirties, but still wearing his flat cap and shorts.

'Extree, extree, *Star Wars* becomes highest grossing film of the year, which is 1977!'

'Now that's more like it!' Trump exclaimed, taking in his surroundings.

'You know this place?' said the Spirit.

'Know it?' said Trump. 'Damn right I know it: this is Fezziwig's! I used to come here all the time when I was a young real estate mogul.'

The pair turned to face the dance floor, over which hung a vast neon sign. Its pink, flashing letters confirmed that this was, indeed, Fezziwig's.

'Unbelievable!' cried Trump, his voice filled with delight. 'This must be the big Christmas shindig!'

'Indeed it is,' replied the Spirit. 'I guess that's why every surface is covered in fake snow.'

'That isn't snow,' said Trump, 'believe me …'

Trump wandered across the dance floor as John Travolta roller-skated by to the strains of 'Jungle Boogie', hand-in-hand with Jimmy Carter.

'Everything's just how I remember,' he marvelled. 'Man, I loved the seventies. The music, the outfits, the glitter balls. Plus you could say all kinds of stuff to women 'cos sexism hadn't been invented yet.'

The Spirit took advantage of his invisibility to glance down a female reveller's dress, once again biting his lower lip.

'Goddamn, if I wasn't a married ghost …'

He turned back to Trump with a look of envy.

'This place is wild,' said the Spirit. 'You must've got a lot of action with a lot of groovy chicks.'

'Well no, actually, cos back then I was with …' Here Trump faltered.

'I don't want to talk about it,' he snapped.

'Suit yourself,' the Spirit replied. 'Why don't we grab a chair?'

Suddenly, Trump froze. You might have said his face drained of all colour, were it not for the permanent coat of mahogany.

'Wait a minute,' he groaned. 'Christmas eve, 1977 … That's when …'

Trump wheeled around and attempted to strike the Spirit, but his little fist could make no contact.

'I know why you brought me here!' he yelped.

The Spirit did not answer, but rather clasped Trump's shoulders in an iron grip, and marched him towards a private booth, in which sat a young couple eating crab linguini. The man was Trump — that was clear enough — and yet how different he looked in his prime! Free of that hulking paunch and bunched up neck-flesh, and with a blond bouffant that was all his own, you might have almost said he was handsome. However, the greatest change was in Trump's expression. Gone were the unfocused glare and duck-like pout, and in their place stood something halfway human. But, oh, how piteous was his lovely companion! She wore a cocktail dress of funeral black, and the tears that filled her eyes caused them to sparkle like glitter balls.

'Belle!' said Trump, though the name caught in his throat.

'Oh baby,' said the Ghost, 'Slick Willy likes what he sees.'

'Hey!' cried Trump. 'That's my fiancée!'

'Not for long …' the Spirit replied, and gestured at the two lovers.

'But I don't understand,' young Trump was pleading. 'Everything's great between us. I take you to the classiest restaurants, we have the most luxurious vacations … I got you a superb engagement ring, the finest platinum. Nobody's seen a diamond like that before, believe me! Why would you want to break things off?'

Belle removed the ring he had mentioned and placed it on the table before him.

'For the reason you have just now illustrated,' she said. 'Ebenezer, your world has become one monstrous spreadsheet!'

'Oh, I get it,' the young Trump muttered. 'Having money's great, but when a guy goes after it, that makes him greedy. Let me tell you something, sweetheart: life is made up of winners and losers, and what you call greed is nothing but a refusal to be the latter!'

'You sell the world short,' she answered, gently. 'You have come to care only for outward splendour, the pantomime of success. You are losing your heart piece by piece, and soon you will have hollowed yourself out entirely. Then I shall be just another accessory to you, no more valued than a sports car or Brioni suit, and as readily replaced.'

'That's not true,' said Trump, without much conviction, for he was not yet the liar he would become. 'How can you be so cruel?'

'Far crueller to have you deny your nature!' cried Belle. 'You are who you are, Ebenezer, and I release you.'

'But I don't want to be released!' Trump exclaimed. 'Why are you doing this to me? It's totally unfair! Horrible!'

Belle's features were full of sorrow, but her voice maintained its hard-won steadiness.

'I do not say these words in anger, but with profound sadness for the love that was once between us. It is for that love's sake that I wish you the best of fortunes. May you fill the world with hotels and casinos and luxury resorts. May you raise your skyscrapers to the very heavens. May you enjoy every accolade and trapping of celebrity that your soul requires. Truly, dear Ebenezer, I hope you are happy in the life you have chosen.'

With that, she departed. The young Trump put his head in his hands, and his entire frame was wracked with sobs.

'Why the hell are you showing me this crap?' Trump cried. 'I want to go home this instant!'

'Keep watching,' said the Spirit.

The younger Trump continued to weep in his linguini. Eventually, a waiter approached him.

'Are you all right, sir?'

Young Trump looked up, his features congealed in a scowl.

'Am I all right? I'm sitting here in a thousand-dollar suit and you ask if I'm all right? How dare you suggest I could be anything other than amazing! You know what? I'm gonna talk to your manager and have you fired.'

'Pardon?'

'You heard me: YOU'RE FIRED!'

Trump and the Spirit surveyed this unhappy scene. After some time had passed, the former spoke in a soft, low voice: 'That was the moment I decided to spend my life grabbing pussy and marrying Eastern European immigrants several decades my junior …'

Sure enough, his younger self had wandered across to the bar, where he ogled a go-go dancer while lighting cigars with hundred-dollar notes. For the first time — perhaps ever — Trump looked circumspect.

'Look, Spirit, I've had enough, all right? Take me back to my bed and my eighty-inch plasma screen.'

'One shadow more!' said the Ghost.

'Unbelievable!' cried Trump. 'This whole thing is rigged!'

Suddenly the walls of the nightclub began to crumble, and green saplings forced themselves through the dance floor. Within moments these had grown into towering elms, which shed their leaves and were covered with snow and cool winter light. Trump blinked, listening to the muffled sound of nearby traffic.

'Hey, I know where we are!' he said. 'We're in Central Park, just next to Fifth Avenue! But what year is it?'

At this point, a cyclist sped past. Strapped to his back was a speaker, from which issued the words: *'Don't cha wish your girlfriend was hot like me? Don't cha wish your girlfriend was a freak like me?'* A man in a tie-dyed crop top walked by, talking on a Motorola about his boyfriend, who hadn't been the same since coming home from Iraq.

Exiting the park, Trump once again spotted the paperboy, sat outside a branch of Starbucks. Now old and grey, he shared his table with a sharp-suited businessman, who was sipping an iced latte.

'I can't believe it,' said the paperboy. 'You're firing me on Christmas Eve? After everything I've done for the company?'

'I'm sorry, Frank,' said the businessman, 'there's just no call for paperboys in 2005, which is the year this is.'

'Oh wow,' said Trump to the Spirit eventually. 'It's 2005? Finally, a happy memory! I was on top of the world back then. *The Apprentice* was killing everybody in the ratings. Yooooooge success.'

'Success,' said the Ghost, 'is in the eye of the beholder. Let's take another look, shall we?'

Soon they had arrived at Trump Tower, that phallic affront to the New York skyline. They passed by security quite unseen, and, after a quick ride of the golden elevator, found themselves on the twenty-sixth floor, in Ebenezer's office. The walls were plastered with magazine covers, each of which sported a grinning Trump. The shelves were laden with self-awarded trophies, and the cluttered desk showed no sign of any work having been done on it. There, behind the desk, sitting in his executive chair, was the Trump we all know and hate: the absurd, urine-yellow sweep of hair; the joyless, porcine squint; the jut-jawed perma-scowl of a third-rate Churchill tribute act.

Before him stood a tall, slender figure; less a woman than some cloistered teen's idea of one. How high were her cheekbones, how lustrous her hair, how perfectly feminine her bearing! And yet, for all that, there was something of Trump about her, in the narrowed slits of her mouth and eyes. It was as though the man had impressed upon her a certain Trumpness, an unmistakable Trumpery, a horrific Trumpitude! Yes, there was no doubt about it: her beauty had been trumped by Trump!

'Melania!' exclaimed the modern Trump. 'We were newlyweds back then. Amazing chemistry. Did it every night, in both positions.'

'It's funny,' said the Spirit, 'you two really don't have the vibe of a married couple. She seems kind of cold towards you.'

'What?' said the aged billionaire. 'Melania's crazy for Trump, believe me.'

His gaze returned to his former self, who was in the process of making a phone call.

'Tell Mr Depp it's his old friend Ebenezer Trump. What? Of course we're friends: we talked for ten whole seconds at the *GQ* awards! Just let Johnny know I look forward to seeing him tonight. At his party, where d'you think? What do you mean I'm not on the guest list? Listen buddy, you get me on that thing, or I will sue you so fast your head will spin!'

He slammed down the receiver as hard as his little hand could manage, then turned his chair to face Melania.

'Sorry babe,' he said, 'was just wrapping up a big deal. Yooooge. They thought they could negotiate with Trump, but, in the end, no one can resist me.'

He started from his chair, his lips puckered, but the Slovene recoiled with a shudder.

'Y'know,' said the Spirit of Clinton, 'I'm maybe not the best marriage counsellor, but that doesn't seem great.'

Arms folded, Melania turned away from her husband.

'Ebenezer,' she said, 'you know deal: three thousand dollar handbag for me to kiss you on mouth.'

He slumped back in his chair, defeated.

'OK, sure, maybe later ...'

After a beat, Trump thought of his recently concluded business.

'Got any plans tonight?' he asked. 'Cos Johnny Depp wants me to come to his Christmas party — begged me, to be honest. Begged. Like a dog. You could come with?'

'No,' replied Melania, 'I am busy this evening. I am going to take shower.'

'What?' cried Trump, incredulous. 'You've already had five this morning! It's like, every time you speak to me, you need to go take a shower...'

'Is just coincidence,' she said, her cat-like eyes shifting from side to side.

'Well then,' he wheedled, 'maybe I could join in sometime?'

Melania shuddered so hard it might have registered on the Richter scale, This done, she departed, leaving the Trump of yesteryear to his magazines and trophies.

'Ugh, not good,' said the Trump of the present. 'C'mon, Spirit, why don't you show me a nice Christmas? Something sweet and mushy and all that crap.'

'Your wish is my command,' said Clinton, and the office fell away in the blink of an eye.

Trump found himself confronted by as tender a tableau of familial love as you might ever care to see. A woman in her late fifties sat at the dining table and gossiped with her adult daughter, while all around them a horde of grandchildren giggled, cavorted and yelled. Oh, this was a fine brood — not for them the gilded opulence of Trump Tower, but rather a humble, cosy, homely home. And how happy it seemed to make them!

'I recognise the daughter,' said Trump. 'I think I ogled her at a beauty pageant once.'

'That's a good guess,' responded the Spirit, 'but no. Check out the mother.'

Trump redirected his squint, then yelped with recognition.

'My God!' he cried. 'It's Belle! Yes, that woman is Belle, as lovely as ever!'

'Isn't she a bit old for you?' said the Spirit, in a sly tone.

'Well, yeah,' said Trump. 'But she looks nice. Y'know, like herself …'

Moving closer to the table, and away from those caterwauling children, Trump overheard the pair's conversation.

'Tell me, dear,' said Belle, 'are you enjoying your liberal arts degree?'

'No Mom,' replied the daughter. 'My whole course is full of sissies and snobs. I think I'm gonna transfer to business school, learn the art of the deal, and make tonnes screwing losers out of their money.'

There emanated from Trump a small, guttural sound, which might have been distant relation to a sob.

'What's the matter?' asked the Ghost.

'Nothing,' Trump responded, wiping his eye. 'I'm just thinking that a kid like that, quite as graceful and as full of promise, might have called me father, and been a spring-time in the haggard winter of my life.'

The Spirit bowed his head.

'That's beautiful,' he said. 'Hey, wait: don't you have five children of your own?'

'Yeah, but three of them are write-offs. Maybe four.'

Just then, the master of the house burst in from the living room, red-faced and clutching his ribs.

'Belle,' cried her husband, right merrily, 'you'll never guess who just came on the television!'

'I don't suppose I shall,' she tutted, 'if you will not deign to tell me.'

'Why,' the man continued, ''tis an old friend of yours!'

'How should I know?' she said, laughing as he laughed, then added in the same breath: 'Mr Trump?'

'Mr Trump it is! He appears to be hosting a game show where suit-wearing cretins pretend he's a genius in the hope that one day they might fetch him coffee! And, as if that wasn't hilarious enough, his face is made up to look like an Oompa Loompa!'

Belle chuckled, then quickly restrained herself.

'Poor Ebenezer. You shouldn't make fun of him so.'

'I don't see what cause you have to call him poor,' said the husband, sitting beside his wife and throwing his arm around her. 'Indeed, he is famously the opposite! I fear I shall have to reserve my sympathy for those who struggle as we do, rather than spend it on a billionaire-cum-reality-show-host!'

'Still,' said Belle, 'I have known him, and thus I understand that, beneath it all, he is the saddest man alive.'

Her point made, she smiled faintly, then acknowledged that, yes, the fake tan *was* ridiculous. And as for that hairpiece …

Trump turned to the shade of Bill Clinton, a tear running down his orange cheek.

'Spirit!' he said in a broken voice. 'Remove me from this place.'

'I told you these were shadows of the things that have been,' said the Ghost. 'That they are what they are, do not blame me!'

'Why do you show me these things?' Trump exclaimed. 'You want me to apologise for who I am, is that it? Well, is it? Damn it, Bill, answer me!'

But the Ghost had vanished, as had Belle and her family, and Trump was back in his bedroom, all alone.

STAVE III

The Second of the Three Spirits

Trump lumbered back to bed and pulled the sheets over himself by way of defence. Though he was greatly wearied by his recent excursion, sleep remained a cold and distant stranger. 'You will be haunted by three Spirits' — that was what Nixon had said. Having been so alarmed by the first, Trump trembled to imagine what form the second would take. He lay there an hour, expecting that any moment the sheets would be torn back and his body exposed like an unwrapped Twinkie. Eventually, Trump's peevishness overcame his terror, and he resolved to deny this ghoul the pleasure of unveiling him. He sprang out of bed with an almighty cry, only to discover that the room was empty.

Empty, perhaps, but not quite silent. As he squinted through the gloom, Trump could hear a noise, distant at first, but growing ever closer. It sounded for all the world like the chanting of an enormous crowd: 'Yes, we can!' the voices called. 'Yes, we can!'

'What the hell?' Trump murmured, for this chorus came not from his TV set, nor the radio nearby, but rather seemed to emanate from the next room. The chant grew louder and louder: 'Yes, we can! YES, WE CAN!'

Trump threw open the door, to stand gawping in amazement. This was his room, all right, but what a transformation had been wrought! It was bathed in a rainbow of light and strewn with brightly coloured streamers. In the centre of it all stood a rangy, hand-some figure, with elephantine ears and a megawatt smile. Why, it was none other than Barack Obama, wearing a Hawaiian shirt and sipping rum from a coconut, a flowery garland hung round his neck!

'Ebenezer!' he cried. 'Come on in!'

Such was Trump's astonishment that it over-whelmed his general desire to do the opposite of whatever he was told, and so he entered.

'As you can see,' said the big-eared intruder, 'I'm uhhhh … enjoying my retirement. Nonetheless, it's important to keep busy, so I'm doing my bit as the, uhhhh, Ghost of Christmas Present.'

'Barack, wow,' said Trump. 'I can't believe you came all the way from Kenya.'

Obama's smile faded then reappeared, like a moon briefly covered by clouds.

'Uhhhh, Mr President … We've been through this extensively. My father was Kenyan, but I myself was born in Hawaii. In fact, I provided the media with my birth certificate.'

'You seem pissed off,' said Trump. 'Hey, I get it: this time of year must be tough for you, seeing as you're a Muslim.'

'For God's—' the Spirit began, then thought better of it. 'Uhhhh, look … I understand that my colleague, the Ghost of, uhhhh, Christmas Past has conjured some visions and taught you a valuable lesson.'

'Not really,' said Trump. 'I'm not much of a learner.'

'Well, nonetheless,' said the Ghost, 'I'm here to show you how other people are spending their holiday.'

'Ugh, fine,' Trump responded. 'Let's get it over with, I guess.'

All at once, they were engulfed in a tremendous snowstorm (though Trump could have sworn that every window was closed) and soon the room had disappeared completely.

The two now stood in a vast square covered in white. Above them, the gorgeous domes of St Basil's Cathedral shone like baubles on a Christmas tree. Everywhere they looked, members of the Bolshoi Ballet leapt and pirouetted, while old, bearded men discussed life under Stalin. Nearby, a couple of Cossacks danced to that music from *Tetris*.

'Where the hell are we?' Trump demanded.

'I thought you, of all people, would recognise it,' said the Spirit. 'We're, uhhhh, in Moscow.'

'Moscow?' repeated Trump. 'Why? If I want to know what's going on in Russia, I can use my secret backchannel.'

Here he paused a moment, and looked anxious.

'Wait a minute, ghost dreams aren't admissible in court, are they?'

'Don't worry, Ebenezer,' the Spirit replied. 'I'm not here to dispense mortal justice, but to save your immortal soul.'

'Yeah, good luck with that,' said Trump.

Rather than respond, the Spirit slipped an arm around him and carried Trump up to the sky. Together they soared above the powdered city, before swooping down towards the Kremlin.

Passing through the walls in a manner that, had they known about it, would have greatly upset Russian Intelligence, the pair traversed the corridors unseen. Eventually they came to a magnificently appointed dining room, where a feast was taking place. At the head of the crowded table, piled high with Christmas fare, there glowered a man of pallid skin and lupine features.

'Vladimir Putin!' Trump squealed boyishly, 'Good guy! Strong leader!'

'Y'know,' said the Spirit, 'I've never understood why you're so keen on the guy. Be honest: does he have some shit on you?'

'Not shit,' said Trump, 'but you're in the right ballpark ...'

Just then, Putin began to tap his glass with a KGB pinkie ring, and the room fell silent.

'Ladies and gentlemen,' he announced, 'as you know too well, I have not always enjoyed a great relationship with journalists, or my political opponents. However, Christmas is a time for us to put aside our differences, which is why I have invited you here to dine at my table.'

Trump furrowed his brow.

'If they're speaking Russian, how come I understand what they're saying?'

'Seriously?' said the Spirit. 'That's the bit that freaks you out? You're being haunted by, uhhhh, literal ghosts!'

'My friends,' Putin continued, 'let us drink to a more peaceful future for our beloved country. *Nostrovia!*'

'*Nostrovia!*' repeated the assembled journalists and politicians, all draining their glasses. Within seconds, each was clutching his or her throat and collapsing upon the table, white foam bubbling from their lips. Putin grinned and helped himself to Christmas pudding as he waited for the twitching to subside.

The Spirit turned to find Trump swaying back and forth on his heels like a toddler.

'I'm bored,' he said.

'How can you be bored?' the Spirit responded. 'We just watched the Russian president murder a roomful of people!'

'Meh,' said Trump. 'I'll believe it when I see it.'

'You just did!'

A sinister, thin-lipped attendant came up to Putin and cast his eyes about the scene of destruction.

'Congratulations, sir,' he said. 'That was masterfully done.'

'Thank you, Sergei Grigorovich.'

'I presume you wish to celebrate, perhaps with a funny movie?'

'Da,' said Putin. 'It is time for another screening of the pee tape.'

The attendant nodded with great solemnity.

'I will bring popcorn.'

'All right,' said Trump, 'I get the picture. Let's go.'

The Spirit gave a mischievous smile. 'You sure? You don't want to see this tape?'

'I said let's go!' said Trump, sweating and tugging at his collar.

As swiftly as a candle is extinguished, the opulence around them disappeared, and Trump found himself standing in a modest but proud household.

'The hell?' he murmured.

'Uhhh,' said the Spirit, 'We're not in Moscow anymore. This is Kansas.'

In the middle of the room, Trump could see a family gathered around a laptop: a father, a mother and their little son.

'What am I looking at?' he demanded.

'Another kind of Christmas,' said the Spirit. 'That's Nader, Shadi and little Jamshid, a family of Muslim-Americans.'

'WRONG!' said Trump. 'Those aren't Muslims. Where are the beards? Where's the ISIS recruitment booth? I don't see a single person firing an AK at the sky.'

'Come on, Ebenezer,' the Spirit admonished, 'you can't generalise like that. There are 1.8 billion Muslims in the world, a quarter of the population.'

'Well, I guess you'd know,' said Trump, 'what with you being one.'

'I swear to God,' the Spirit snapped, 'if you don't shut your damn mouth, I'll uhhhh ... kick your ass!'

After a beat, the Spirit lowered his head and massaged his temples.

'I'm sorry,' he said. 'I pride myself on being the calmest person on earth, but, man, you get to me. The point is, the Najafis here may not be Christian, but they're still spending the holiday together as a family. Well, not the whole family ...'

At this point, the plangent ring of Skype was heard and a kindly old woman appeared on the laptop.

'*Maman bozorg!*' Jamshid cried, '*Maman bozorg!*' and chattered away so rapidly that his parents had to remind him to breathe.

'That's Jamshid's grandma,' said the Spirit. 'He's saying he wishes more than anything that she were here.'

'Why isn't she?' asked Trump. 'Husband wouldn't let her out the house?'

'Don't you remember?' replied the Spirit. 'You signed a travel ban. What was it you called for? "A total and complete shutdown of Muslims entering

the United States until our country's representatives can figure out what's going on"?'

'Sure,' said Trump, 'but I didn't mean old ladies. I meant, y'know, *Muslim* Muslims ... The terror guys.'

'Do you even know the first thing about the Middle East?' the Spirit demanded. 'The difference

between Sunni and Shia? Salafi and Wahhabi inter-
pretations of Islam? The current conflict in Yemen,
in which Saudi forces are backing President Abdrab-
buh Mansour Hadi against a Houthi rebellion?'

A look of doubt crept across Trump's features.

'I ... I ... To be honest, I don't really care about
Muslims. I just said that stuff to get applause at
my rallies. And the tougher I was, the more applause
I got.'

He turned back to the family, who gazed at their
distant loved one through the laptop screen.

'Maybe I'll rethink the ban,' said Trump. 'The
alt-right won't like it, but, then again, those guys
never leave their parents' basements, so who cares?'

The Spirit gave a small nod, and the room
was gone.

In less than a moment they were back in Washington. Trump now faced an underpass, within
which huddled a crowd of the destitute.

'What do you think of that?' said the Spirit.

'Horrible   construction   job,'   he   replied.
'Should've got me to do it. Nobody knows more
about infrastructure than Trump.'

'I was talking about the people inside it.'

'Oh.'

They walked beneath the concrete arch and Trump sneered at the homeless, quivering in their sleeping bags.

'Sad!' he exclaimed. 'Pathetic! A mess!'

'No roaring hearth for them this Christmas,' mused the Spirit. 'Of course, there are those who could help ... How much did you say you were worth? Ten billion dollars?'

'Hey, it's not my fault these guys are losers,' said Trump. 'I'm rich cos I earned it. If they can't be bothered to succeed, they should just die and stop wasting my air.'

'You know, there's more to life than winners and losers,' remonstrated the Ghost.

'Wrong!' Trump returned. 'This world's like *The Apprentice*: the strong get ahead and the weak get canned.'

Here, the Spirit rounded on Trump, his giant ears enflamed with anger.

'Uhhhh, look,' he said, 'you claim you want to make America great again, but you know what really stops America being great? It's guys like you, who are born with everything and refuse to relinquish one bit of it! They hoard their wealth, dodge their taxes, and pay politicians to remove any obstacles in their way. Then, on top of all that, they lecture those born with nothing on responsibility! Well, what about your responsibility? To those the system fails? To those you exploit? To the future generations you'll screw over till your dying day?'

As he took this in, Trump noticed a change in the Spirit's appearance: his handsome face was lined with wrinkles, and his hair had turned quite grey.

'Wow, Barack,' said Trump. 'All due respect, you look like crap.'

'I am nearing the end of my term,' sighed the Spirit. 'Whoever said black don't crack clearly didn't have to deal with jackasses like you ... Nonetheless, we have one last site to visit.'

The Ghost led Trump through the snowy streets until they found themselves upon the threshold of a humble dwelling

'Geez, what a dump,' said Trump. 'Whose house is this?'

'A man materially poor but rich in affection,' said the Spirit. 'You know him well, or, rather, you see him often.'

'Hey,' Trump replied, 'if I wanted a brainteaser, I'd try reading my healthcare Bill.'

Well, who should come bustling up to the door just then, but Trump's trusty aide, Bob Cratchit? That honest man was quite laden with presents, and upon his shoulder sat his son, who carried a crutch, and whose limbs were supported by an iron frame.

'Tell me, Li'l Marco,' Bob Cratchit cried, 'how do you think these gifts shall be received by your brothers and sisters?'

'They shall be received right joyfully!' the child exclaimed, in a sweet, small voice. 'And how blessed are we, who are given the chance to bring such joy!'

The door was opened by Mrs Cratchit, a brave, sturdy, good-hearted woman, who greeted her husband with a kiss as Trump and the Spirit pursued him inside.

In a matter of seconds, Bob was set upon and besieged by the massed army of his offspring, who plundered the presents from his arms and clambered all over him as though he were a jungle gym. Once tolerably assured their father had had enough, they hustled the boy, and bore him off to the kitchen, that he might hear the pudding singing in the copper.

'How did Li'l Marco behave?' asked Mrs Cratchit.

'Oh, he was a perfect angel,' said Bob. 'You should have seen how he rejoiced in the singing of carollers, and pled that I should give his presents to children poorer than he.'

Upon this account, Mrs Cratchit's eyes fair brimmed with tears.

'How dear a child God has granted us,' she sniffed, 'and how wretched we shall be if he is taken away!'

'The hell's she talking about?' Trump asked the Spirit.

'Li'l Marco is seriously ill,' he replied. 'And since you dismantled Obamacare, the Cratchits can no longer afford his treatment.'

'My God,' Trump exhaled, 'I had no idea.'

Trump and the Spirit followed the Cratchits into their living room, where the children were violently engaged in a game of cops and protestors. However, Li'l Marco soon erupted in a fit of coughs and, when he removed the handkerchief from his mouth, it was flecked with blood.

'Oof,' said Trump. 'Not good.'

Mrs Cratchit caught Bob by the arm and took him to one side.

'Enough is enough, Bob Cratchit,' said that formidable woman. 'Our son is wasting away for want of money while you toil each day for that rich old rogue. You march into his Oval Office first thing tomorrow and demand that he help us.'

'My dear,' said Bob, 'that would never work. I should be fired before uttering the words "may I".'

'What?' cried Trump, bewildered. 'Why would Bob think I wouldn't help him in his hour of need?!'

'Mr Trump is forever telling me,' said Cratchit, 'that if I should ever have an hour of need, I'd better stay the hell away from him.'

'Oh, that villain!' his good wife cried. 'Who would deny decent wages to a man whose son is on the brink of —'

Here she glanced down, for Li'l Marco was tugging upon the hem of her apron.

'Please, mother,' the lad chirruped, 'do not speak ill of our beloved president, for I know he must be a good man, and taken up with matters far greater than a young cripple.'

'Spirit,' said Trump, with an interest he had never felt before, 'tell me if Li'l Marco will live.'

The Ghost's visage was grim as he gazed upon the Cratchits: 'If these shadows remain unaltered by the Future, the child will die.'

'No! No!' cried Trump. 'Horrible! Sad!'

'Why should you care?' the Spirit responded in an icy tone. 'It's not your fault these guys are losers.'

'But Bob's a good man!' said Trump. 'He breaks his back every day, and all I do is abuse him. Wow, it's almost as though your wealth isn't directly proportional to how hard you work, or how good you are as a person ...'

Suddenly, those beady eyes lit up with inspiration.

'Wait, I can help — I'm super rich and I only ever spend it on garbage! I don't need a gold toilet! I don't need to light my cigars with hundred-dollar bills — a fifty burns just as well! Oh Bob, Bob, please let me save him!'

Alas, neither Cratchit nor his family could heed these words. Indeed, no sooner were they spoken than the scene before Trump's eyes began to fade. He looked about him for the Ghost, but saw it not. Suddenly, he became conscious of a dreadful sound — the tolling of an unseen bell. Three Spirits, Trump thought; that's what Old Dick Nixon had promised. He turned, with no small reluctance, to behold a solemn Phantom, draped and hooded, coming, like a mist along the ground, towards him.

STAVE IV

The Last of the Spirits

'What do you want, you spooky prick?!' cried Trump.

The tall Spectre approached in silence, looking down at him with invisible eyes.

'What's with the hood?' Trump asked. 'I'm guessing some kind of Black Lives Matter thing? Cos I don't go in for that, all right? As far as I'm concerned, the only life that matters is mine.'

The Spirit continued to stare. Trump, who usually loved nothing more than the sound of his own voice, found himself craving a dialogue. He pressed on: 'We've had the Ghost of Christmas Past, and the Ghost of Christmas Present, so what are you, the Ghost of Christmas Yet to Come?'

Again, there came no reply.

'Oh great,' said Trump, 'the silent treatment. You must be one of my wives. Well, none of them are yet to come, believe me.'

The Spirit resumed its wordless advance.

'Look, whatever you're planning, there's no need, OK? I've learned my lesson: give a little to charity, be nicer to A-rabs, yada yada yada.'

It raised a bony hand.

'All right, listen!' yelled Trump. 'I'm a dealmaker! I make deals, great deals. If you can see your way clear to letting this go, I'll make it worth your while. You could be ambassador to Denmark. Bermuda, even!'

The Ghost gripped his shoulder and all was darkness.

When Trump came to, an acrid scent assailed him. They were in Washington, though that name did not seem appropriate for the desolation he beheld. Getting up, Trump grimaced at the burnt-out buildings and smouldering mounds of rubble. On one of these piles sat the paperboy, now horribly wizened, with a long, white beard. He cackled hysterically and cried, 'Oh God, why have you cursed me to live in 2025, which is the year this is?!'

'Eesh,' said Trump, 'the guy who came after me must have really screwed the pooch.'

He and the Spirit trudged through the abandoned streets, and everywhere was strewn with ancient litter and the charred remains of the dead.

'Guh,' said Trump, 'can't say I'm loving this. Depressing!'

After a while, he stopped and brightened somewhat.

'Now that I like!'

They were now in sight of the Washington Monument, which had somehow survived this catastrophe. However, there now stood alongside it a golden obelisk, twice as tall and of far greater girth. At its base was a sign, which read 'THE TRUMP MONUMENT — I GUARANTEE YOU THERE'S NO PROBLEM. I GUARANTEE'. Trump would have stopped to admire the impressive erection, but for the Spirit placing a bony hand on his shoulder and compelling him onwards.

They walked through the ruins for what seemed to Trump an eternity, the Spirit never uttering a word.

'I think I've figured this out,' he said. 'You're Jim Comey, right? There can't be that many eight-foot freaks who have it in for me ...'

At that point, Trump glimpsed a feeble light, which battled the surrounding gloom. Moving towards it, he saw a group of survivors sat around a campfire, their eyes sunken and faces gaunt.

The leader, a man who could have been anything from sixteen to sixty, had impaled a rat on a sharpened stick, which he held above the flames.

'Trump,' he croaked, his voice heavy with despair. 'We all thought he was funny to begin with. A harmless idiot. Well, he may have been an idiot, but he was far from harmless. And now the joke's on us ...'

'Tell me,' said a child covered in grime, 'how did he bring about the Day of Judgement, the Fire that Scorched the Skies?'

A bitter laugh sprang from the leader's lips. 'He started a Twitter beef with the prime minister of Belgium. Something about who had the bigger shoe size. One thing led to another and, before we knew it, we were in an all-out nuclear war with Europe. But, to be honest, the country was ruined long before the bombs dropped. He turned all our national parks into strip malls. Knocked the libraries down to build Trump casinos. Changed the name of every day to "Trumpday", so that no one knew when anything was.'

'OK,' said Trump to the Spirit, 'it does kinda sound like I messed up. Not all bad, though: did you hear the part about the casinos?'

Having grilled the rat to his liking, the leader tore it into pieces, which he passed around the circle.

'Are all people as wretched as us?' asked the child, while taking a bite.

'Not everyone,' his elder replied. 'As ever, the wealthy were able to take care of themselves. They rode out the apocalypse in Sector T, a gated community in which they thrive to this day. The screen-swipers! The kale-eaters! They go everywhere in their Ubers, which is why they call themselves the Ubermen ...'

'Still,' said the child, 'we are fortunate indeed to to eat rat. Why do you grant us this luxury?'

The leader bowed his head. 'Because,' he said, 'in times gone by, this was a day of celebration. I want you to know some fraction of the joy I had at your age. And so, I say to you, child: Merry Christmas—'

At this point, the tip of a spear exploded through the man's chest, and he slumped face-first onto the fire.

'WHOA!' yelled Trump, as a hail of arrows sent the survivors scurrying in each direction.

'The red hats are coming!' cried the child. 'THE RED HATS ARE COMING!'

All around them could be heard the sound of sinister war-cries: 'MAGA!' and 'BILDAWOLL!'

Out of the darkness came a pack of men wearing frog masks and baseball caps. 'MAGA!' they shrieked, as they shook their spears: 'BILDAWOLL!'

Most of the group were struck down attempting to flee; those unlucky enough to be captured were returned to the campsite.

'What should we do with these cucks?' asked one of the marauders.

'That's a decision for the High Priest,' replied another.

From the shadows stepped an old man covered in pelts, whose staff was topped with a human skull. As he paused to inspect the survivors, a Frog called out: 'What is thy bidding, Lord Gingrich?'

'We shall sacrifice this child to the Orange God,' said the old man, in a reedy voice. 'The rest shall be eaten.'

The marauders whooped and cheered. 'MAGA!' they yelled. 'MAGA! MAGA!'

The High Priest turned and raised his staff to the heavens: 'My friends, we may not have clean water, but tonight we shall drink liberal tears!'

This elicited from the crowd a deafening roar, over which Trump could hear a voice cry, 'Bring out the creature!'

A cage was opened and onto the ground sprawled a naked thing with bleached blond hair and a string of pearls, which capered and writhed in the dirt.

'Milo is your friend!' it said, clutching at the marauders' legs. 'Milo loveses the Orange God as much as you, yes he doesssss!'

'Shut up, limey!' yelled a marauder, and knocked the creature to the ground.

'Yesssss!' Milo cried. 'Beat me, beat me, just give me your attention, pleasssssssssse!'

The High Priest drew a ceremonial blade and ordered the child be brought forward.

'My fellow Deplorables,' he intoned, 'it is written in the Book of Tweets that Fake News CNN and the failing *New York Times* did anger the Orange God, which is why, in His wisdom, He purged our land with fire. But if we praise His name and offer Him sacrifice, He shall walk among us and make America great again AGAIN!'

Trump turned to the Spirit, not a little perturbed.

'Wow,' he said, 'this isn't what I wanted. I just wanted to be on TV all the time and for everyone to respect me. Honestly? This doesn't feel great. I've got this weird pain in my chest — like I'm feeling bad, but for other people?'

The Spirit was as still as a statue.

'Then again,' Trump continued, 'there's got to be an upside. Let's have a look at that Sector T place, the one the guy mentioned before he ... y'know ...'

At this, the Spirit grasped his arm and the campsite evaporated.

The two now stood before the gleaming gates of an apartment complex, whose holographic sign read 'SECTOR T — SPONSORED BY FACEBOOK'. They passed through the insubstantial bars and walked along a promenade lined with coffee shops and Apple Stores. A pair of millennials strolled past.

'Giving this nuclear holocaust serious side-eye, hashtag shade,' said one.

'THIS. IS. NOT. NORMAL,' said the other, clapping between each word.

'Nice place,' said Trump. 'Clean. But wait, if it's Christmas, where are all the decorations? The merry revellers? Surely some people must be celebrating?'

The Spirit turned its hood towards an open door, from which emanated the sound of electronic music and glad young voices. With a sweep of its arm, it bade Trump enter.

Hipsters! Hipsters everywhere! Hipsters dancing to an indie playlist coming from an iPhone in its speaker dock. Hipsters vaping on every flavour of e-liquid, from ocean lime to strawberry banana waffle. Hipsters checking their privilege and debating whether Lena Dunham was problematic. All around Trump was a whirl of man-buns and nose-rings, of pussy hats and Black Lives Matter shirts, of ironic tattoos and non-binary pronouns.

'Oof, not my kind of party,' he said. 'Way too ethnic. And none of the girls are wearing dresses!'

At that point, the iPhone was unplugged from its speaker and the room fell silent. A woman in plaid held her craft beer aloft.

'A toast!' she cried. 'To the happy corpse, may he rot in pieces!'

'Whoa,' said Trump, 'they're celebrating someone's death? That's pretty dark. Whoever this guy was, he must have been horrible, a real loser. I'm thinking, Alec Baldwin?'

'I'll give him one thing,' continued a young man with a Dalí moustache, 'he never gladdened a human heart in life, but, by God, his death has brought us joy!'

As though to prove his point, the whole assembly broke out in laughter, and Trump could not help but chip in a chuckle.

'Imagine being so hated,' he said to the Spirit. 'I almost want to see the poor schmuck's funeral.'

No sooner had he spoken than the party was transformed into a grey and dismal cemetery.

Trump now beheld a dry-eyed burial, with but a smattering of mourners. Two businessmen stood close at hand.

'Hell of turnout,' yawned the one. 'I'm surprised anyone showed.'

'I'm only here for the free lunch,' replied the other.

Trump could hear the drone of a eulogy, and, moving closer, he realised it was being given in a slurred British accent. Yes, there was the speaker, cradling his pint and looking like a cirrhotic Mr Toad, his dark suit enlivened by a pair of Union Jack shoes. Trump winced, for it was Nigel Farage.

'Ugh, Jesus,' he said, 'it's that Brexit dude. He's always kissing my ass. Sucks to be the dead guy, if that's the best speaker they could find.'

'A terrible loss,' said Farage, between slurps of bitter. 'He was a great leader, a tremendous businessman, and, speaking personally, my very dearest friend. Oh, by the way, if anyone here from Fox News would like to hire me as a commentator, I'll be around at the reception.'

To one side of the grave stood a slender woman in black. She lifted her veil, disclosing a set of feline features and improbably high cheekbones.

'Melania?' Trump exclaimed. 'What's she doing at some guy's funeral? I explicitly told her she's not to form attachments in this country.'

The Spirit extended a skeletal finger and pointed out the large, gold-plated gravestone, already spattered with bird shit. Though Trump was cognisant of a terrible foreboding, he found himself pulled forth by forces beyond his comprehension. He inched closer and closer, until finally, on the stone of that neglected grave, he read his own name: @EbenezerTrump.

'So I'm the dead guy,' Trump muttered. 'Nice!'

Farage finished his speech, tipped the dregs of his pint over the grave, then lurched his way towards Trump's widow.

''Ullo, love,' he slurred, 'sorry for your loss and all that.'

'Is OK,' Melania replied, 'I do not really give shit. Is just annoying — Ebenezer spend all his money on dumb monument, so now I do not have place to live.'

At this, Farage's grin grew even wider.

'Well, in that case,' he said, 'why don't you kip at mine tonight? Geddit? UKIP at mine?!'

Farage's great red face roared with laughter as he cast an arm around the widow and drunkenly led her away.

'Hey!' Trump cried. 'That's my woman!'

He watched in impotent horror as the pair stepped inside a cab and were driven off.

'Dammit,' he sighed, 'why did I trust that guy? Why would anyone trust him?'

As the last few mourners left the churchyard, Trump stared at the sod, uncharacteristically subdued. Eventually, he turned back to face the Spirit.

'Listen,' he said, 'if you're gonna hit me with death, at least show me one that people give a crap about.'

There was a slight inclination of the Spirit's hood and, all of a sudden, its robes billowed forth in a great wave of black, engulfing Trump.

Having fought his way out the Stygian folds, Trump found himself standing, once more, outside the home of old Bob Cratchit.

'Oh geez,' he said, as cold realisation washed over him. 'C'mon, Spirit, I don't need to see this.'

The Spirit indicated the doorway and, once more, some mystic force compelled Trump forward. There, in the living room, he saw Bob Cratchit. Bob was older, yes, but not enough to warrant those haggard features, nor that bone-white hair. His wife sat nearby, but, oh, what a change in that redoubtable woman! Where all had been hearty and stout, now lay sadness and fragility. Try as she might to distract herself with Sudoku, poor Mrs Cratchit could not but return to some awful memory, which filled her eyes with tears.

'Do not cry, my love,' said Bob. 'At least he was spared the horror of this new world.'

'But he should have weathered it,' she responded, 'for he was the bravest little soul!'

Trump turned to the Spirit.

'My God,' he murmured, 'does this mean …'

Once again, the spectral finger pointed, and Trump's gaze followed. There, above the mantel-piece, hung a tiny, ownerless crutch, a shrine to the child who had once blessed that dwelling.

'Oh, Li'l Marco!' Trump howled, and fell to his knees.

Tears poured from his eyes – and you would not have believed such a deluge could escape those narrow slits! He hammered his chest with tiny fists, then, casting aside his nightcap, tore mighty chunks from his weave.

'Spirit!' Trump cried, tight clutching at its robe. 'Hear me, for I am not the man I was! I see now that my life has been one of folly, of selfishness and humbug; that I have done naught but desecrate this land for my own fruitless gain! Tell me these visions may be reversed, and the future made whole! Give me the chance to do so, to save Li'l Marco and the millions of other children who might suffer like him! Oh Spirit, please take me back! I want to help the world, not just stamp my name on it!'

Holding up his hands in a final prayer, Trump saw an alteration in the Phantom's appearance: its robes shrunk and grew pale, folding in on themselves before collapsing to the floor as a pair of underpants.

STAVE V

The End of It

Picking them up, he could discern a monogram — DJT — and upon the label stood the words 'Trump Collection Briefs — Made in China'. Yes! The underwear was his own! Overjoyed, Trump pressed them to his face (a gesture he instantly regretted). Nonetheless, they were his, and the floor was his, and the whole surrounding room was his. He was back in the White House and everything was just as it had been: indeed, the TV was still blaring out Fox News. Another platinum blonde was holding forth on the causal relationship between gun control and hurricanes. Dazed, Trump grabbed the remote and turned off the monitor.

'Unbelievable!' he said to himself. 'The Spirits have heeded my prayer. Oh, joyous day! Oh, miracle of miracles! I've been given a second chance — a chance to live a life of kindness and decency!'

And so he had! Trump could see his future stretching out before him (as far as it could stretch, given he was a seventy-one-year-old who mainly ate KFC). He skipped and gambolled through his chambers in a transport of delight.

'Thank you, Hillary! Thank you, Richard Nixon! Thank you to every Spirit who worked to instil these better spirits in me! A Merry Christmas to everybody! And, what is more, a Happy New Year! Whoop, I say: whoop and hurrah! Oh, I'm so happy, I don't know what to do!'

Suddenly, a thought struck him and, with a cry, he snatched up his Samsung.

Ebenezer Trump tweeted:
JOY TO THE WORLD! #Christmas #NoHumbug
07.32 — 25 Dec 2017

Ebenezer Trump tweeted:
People shouldn't be dismissed as losers or haters.
We're all part of a family of man, and our duty is to
love one another.
07.32 — 25 Dec 2017

Ebenezer Trump tweeted:

Glad tidings to those of every religion: Jewish,
Muslim, that one with the elephant guy. ALL GOOD!
07.33 — 25 Dec 2017

His mentions were instantly filled with alt-right supporters saying 'WTF?' and calling him a cuck, but Trump cared not. What need had he of the Frogs' adulation, when he knew he spoke his heart? Running over to the window, he threw it open and took a great gulp of vivid winter air. Glancing down, Trump spotted a passing urchin. He briefly paused to wonder why the Secret Service had allowed an urchin onto the White House lawn, but this was no great matter.

'You there!' cried Trump. 'What day is it?'

'Today?' replied the child. 'Why sir, today is Christmas Day!'

'It's Christmas Day!' Trump exclaimed to himself. 'I haven't missed it! The Ghosts have done it all in one night. They can do anything — of course they can! Tremendous Ghosts, the best Ghosts!'

His thoughts returned to the ragamuffin below.

'Hey there, little fella,' he called down, 'you know the Whole Foods just around the corner?'

'I should hope I did,' replied the lad.

'Smart kid!' said Trump. 'Great kid! Remark-able! Do they still have that turkey in the window?'

'What, the one as big as me?' returned the boy.

'That's right!' said Trump. 'It's a big, beautiful turkey, the best, believe me. Yoooooooge. I want you to buy the thing and bring it here. Take my wallet!'

With that, he launched said item out the window and into the urchin's eager grasp.

'That should cover it,' said Trump. 'How much is a turkey these days? Two thousand dollars?'

'Sounds about right,' said the boy, and took off like a shot.

'I'll take it to Bob Cratchit's!' Trump whispered, rubbing those tiny hands with glee. 'Imagine the look upon his face when he sees me! Why, SNL never made a joke such as that!'

He dashed over to the wardrobe and, instead of selecting his customary six-foot tie, took out a regular-sized one. After all, what was he trying to prove? As he threw on his clothes, Trump chuckled to himself and made a thousand cheery plans.

'Henceforth, I shall endeavour to be a better president — ha, it won't be hard! I shall slander and lie no more, but rather use my words to elevate those who hear them. I shall protect the environment, and cherish this globe that blesses us with its munificence. I shan't build walls, but rather tear them down — the walls of poverty, the walls of ignorance, the walls that divide us from our fellow man! Oh, I should call Hillary. I treated her rough during that election. Horrible! I mean, lock her up? C'mon!'

Now fully dressed, he pulled on his overcoat, marvelling at the spot where the Ghost of Nixon had stood.

'Yes,' he exclaimed, 'I shall be a better politician, and, furthermore, I shall strive to be a better man!

I'll spend time with my beloved children: Ivanka, Donald, and the other three! And women! I shall respect women with every fibre of my being. I'll no longer grab 'em by the pussy, but rather grab 'em by the heart! Why stop there? I'll respect everyone on earth: man and woman, rich and poor, black and white, gay and straight, trans and cis! Oh, by the glory of this season, I shall love them all as I have hitherto loved myself!'

With that, he went careening out the residence and bounced along the corridor, hallo-ing and embracing everyone he met!

Those staffers who glimpsed Trump that day marvelled to see a man transformed: he no longer squinted, but widened his eyes to take in the world's delights. In place of his pout stood a broad, receptive smile; his hair still looked like a mutilated alpaca, but, then, one cannot have everything. Emerging from the White House, Trump encountered the urchin, who, good as his word, had secured the vastest turkey in all of Whole Foods (misplacing the man's wallet in the process). But Trump did not mind — how could he, when confronted with a bird so admirably proportioned? He stuffed it into his limo, tousled the boy's hair, then hopped in and cried: 'Driver, take me to the home of old Bob Cratchit!'

'Mr President!' the good man cried, upon answering his door. 'I thought you had granted me this day off work. If I misconstrued, then I do apologise.'

'My dear Bob!' Trump responded. 'You have no cause to be sorry, but rather I must apologise to you! I have been a miser, a slave-driver, a skinflint and a churl!'

'Oh no, sir,' Bob demurred, 'I shouldn't go that far ...'

'I should!' said Trump. 'And a good deal further! But I have changed my ways, and now beseech you to enumerate my former flaws, that I might better avoid them in future.'

'Well,' said Bob, a little tentative, 'I suppose you could have been more generous on occasion. And, from time to time, I may have found you less than courteous ...'

'Come now, man,' Trump laughed, 'I've been a brute and I give you leave to say so. Pray, let me have it!'

'All right,' said Cratchit, taking a deep breath. 'You have been a sexist, a racist and a boor.

You were at once a spoiled infant and a sleazy old man.'

'Yes!' Trump chortled. 'I suppose I was!'

'A vain monster,' Bob continued, 'a vicious clown, a fraud, an ignoramus and a bigot. In fact, if I'm honest, you were a total piece of shi—'

'OK, OK, I get it,' Trump interrupted. 'And though I may never undo those years of ill use, I should like to offer you a well-earned pay rise!'

Mrs Cratchit, who had been eavesdropping on their exchange, could no longer hold her tongue.

'About bloody time!' she cried.

Trump guffawed, a sound that was, until then, as rarely heard as a mermaid's song, or a decent Jay-Z track post-*Black Album*.

'Oh, formidable woman,' he exclaimed, 'dear Bob is fortunate indeed you are willing to fight his corner! It *is* bloody time, just as it's bloody time I volunteered to pay Li'l Marco's medical bills!'

This was all too much for Bob Cratchit, who began to weep with joy.

'God bless you, sir,' said he. 'May the name of Trump be synonymous with kindness, selflessness and charity!'

'My fine fellow,' Trump replied, putting an arm around him, 'I do not crave fame or adulation, merely the knowledge that I have fulfilled my duty to those in need. Now, driver, bring out the turkey!'

The table was laid and the bird was cooked — wonderfully, I should add, for Mrs Cratchit — finest of women! — performed each task to the utmost degree. Trump's turkey occupied pride of place, and the children were unanimous in praising its size, its aroma, and its general excellence. In due course, Bob Cratchit got to his feet and, lifting a glass of port as red as his beaming face, cried, 'To Mr Trump!'

'To Mr Trump!' yelled the Cratchits all, and none louder than Li'l Marco, who jigged lustily in his chair, waving his crutch like a tomahawk.

'Merry Christmas!' he cried. 'God bless the U.S., every one!'

'Mr President,' Bob Cratchit boomed, 'would you do us the honour of slicing the bird?'

'That would be an honour indeed,' said Trump, 'but alas I must leave you.'

'Will you not stay to share our meal?' Li'l Marco protested.

'Would that I could,' Trump said, 'but I am called to another table, that of my daughter Ivanka. I must make amends for spurning her invitation, and for the years I spent perving on her. Not sure what that was about ...'

Trump made his goodbyes, and warmly embraced each Cratchit in turn. He observed once more this scene of familial bliss, then headed for the door. However, as he stepped outside, Trump paused with a troubled expression.

'Wait a minute ...' the billionaire muttered. 'None of this makes any sense. Why would I need to change my ways? I mean, everybody loves me! I'm a good guy, the best guy, I've got the most friends. That's it! Those Ghosts must have been FAKE NEWS! The losers and haters in the mainstream media, trying to stop Trump being number one! Well, to hell with that!'

Trump turned and marched back up to the gathered Cratchits.

'Bob?' he said.

'Yes sir?'

'YOU'RE FIRED!'

'What?' Bob cried, his face draining of its ruddy hue. 'Why?'

'Why?' yelled Trump. 'You've been totally disloyal. Called me a miser, a slave-driver, a skinflint and a churl. So unfair, horrible!'

'Sir,' the poor man protested, 'those were your words!'

'And now you're calling me a liar! Unbelievable!'

Bob Cratchit bowed his head, and said in a small voice: 'I thought you'd learned the error of your ways.'

'WRONG!' Trump bellowed. 'I haven't learned squat — now, gimme that ...'

He scooped up the turkey, knocking Li'l Marco from his chair in the process, then stormed right out of the house. Soon Trump was back in the Oval

Office, lighting a cigar with a hundred-dollar note and resting his feet on the uneaten bird. Leaning back in his chair, he thought of how he might use the New Year to enrich himself at the expense of others, and let out a satisfied murmur. As for Christmas, and its Spirits, and any lesson they wished to convey, well, Trump had a word to sum it all up: 'HUMBUG!'

What to make of this sorry tale? Perhaps its moral shall be that redemption has its limits, or, more simply, that President Trump is, was, and shall be a malicious orange scumbag. Let us hope that the Ghost of Christmas Yet to Come's predictions may not come to pass, and that the man may be removed from office before irrevocable damage is done. Until then, stay safe, be merry, and, as Li'l Marco observed, God bless the U.S., every one!

The End